NATURAL HISTORY
RAPE MUSEUM

Also by Danielle Pafunda

Pretty Young Thing

My Zorba

Iatrogenic: Their Testimonies

Manhater

DANIELLE PAFUNDA

NATURAL HISTORY RAPE MUSEUM

Published by Bloof Books

www.bloofbooks.com

Bloof Books are printed in the USA by Bookmobile. Booksellers, libraries, and other institutions may order direct from us by contacting sales@bloofbooks.com. POD editions are distributed via Ingram, Baker & Taylor, and other wholesalers. Individuals may purchase our books direct from our website, from online retailers such as Amazon.com, or request them from their favorite bookstores.

Please support your local independent bookseller whenever possible.

ISBN: 978-0-9826587-5-8

O N E

T W O

T H R E E

FOUR

FIVE

ETCETERA

ONE

When they called me vagina. When they called themselves screwed.

When they made the father hold ice in his craw

till he yanked. When they gave the mother

a sleek tail and filled her I hated myself in with beetle blood.
your womb from
When they scammed the conception knobs.

When they swaddled me slaughter dander and limp.

When they told me to do what you done and better it,

not take the shine off, keep quiet in there, cotton stuff

my v-able slag hole. To poison.

All my long life they every day loved me

by sticking their fingers into my pudge.

C'mon over here and presh me then. Cootchie-coo my wattle.
Dove curdle and spit it palm.

We have come here to | You put me in this dress, | assemble
our herniated memoir. | I'm just wearing it. | Fat needles,
huffer glue, soap scum | Externally. | fingernail

scraping through the bandage.

Why'd we carry heavy   if it was gonna punch out
our rosy patoot?

Why'd we live   at home   all those years?

We have come here to discuss   the rape death bad mood
of my friend, sister,   twin sister,   that dead girl.

We have come here to look at a series of photographs
made thin by dint of sick glug from the split sass spout.

We have come here   to sign a document
certifying our level of pie hole.

We. The dress and me   got hung up
'round your roping peg.

If you don't like to look at bare sockets   flip up my skirt.

The fuckwad wants to know why she's bothering to dress
like a lady. He notes every article has a drawstring,

a pull tab, insectile | I am boring you to | metal hooks,
adhesive backing, | death; I am boring | running boards,
fretwork, swizzle | into you | sticks.

It'd be better, she imagines, in the formaldehyde top hat.
Better with her beaver-tooth corset cinched 'round her weave.
I am too fat and loose for stuffing, she says.
Too skin and rigid for riding. The fuckwad scooped out her girl bag.
From now on, everything red goes in that gutter, everything

redder

goes toward the slit mouth and dirt clod.

I have once know what you did, she says. *I have once plunked
down your hot tongue and called it leaven. I scour me. I search
for a thread of git. You nod off, you nod me off a' knocking.*

In this sticky ultrapocket, the fuckwad waxes sentimental.

His narcosis, his grandiose flag hag, his busted nose candy

feather-dusted collection, clam-fisted breakfront

lit with a ureic pall. Caved-in bluegrass, toe-tapping

pappy spasm, rim-pinking sound from the caved-in speaker.

In this punky loam | The man in your life | vista, count
the preservations | will exercise his fink | gone wrong.
Pop the glass eye | till it wail | from his mildewed outlet.
Pin to his gagsuit | | lapel a list of history.

A listory: sunshine, mollycoddle, sweetheart, princess,

supine, peep cheater, gosh all git up.

Now you think it's precious tempo? That's his pencil

fugging your plasma right back to basic.

The fuckwad says: My dear, my doughy dewy doe-eyed dimple,

you mustn't attempt to think while you sphinx.

You mustn't | Advice will be heeded | leave the room,

for you haven't | even as you attempt to | ever yet.

And what will | head strong / headstrong | baby-job think?

What will he odious pus

in the empty nest with a piddle of wire and prong?

What will he when he gets in your grill and finds

that you've gone?

Look you after that corset, which strings trick you out

and whip you floss again. Look above you, a halo

to still your rove mag eye. Taken won't you?

With his obliging fig paw? His homeothermic enterprise?

The fuckwad says: Really, a number of wolves?

Think you not actually mice in the gut?

Oughtn't you ignore mice, foul weather,

other shod feet shambling? Whatever the world,

it hasn't called your name. It hasn't lifted your lip.

The fuckwad's translating again: She the dog pets it,

she the dog it | When you lie down you get | pet.

Feeds it with | up again and there are fleas | a supper,

she the dog | as well as bedbugs | walks on a leash.

She the dog | | found by the brook.

She the dog out by the fence.   Mending.

She the dog red supper meat. She the dish full of cigars.

Dog the wolf with teeth from the junker.

Dog the wolf with headful of pace.

Wolfing up on the rag rug, filed to its singular risk.

The tip of its species, and the shiv of the world.

But the fuckwad sings it: I'd rather my itch scratch

than bed down the cur/b.

Each slick grim slab cue each damp day rain gray cement symmetrical ceremonial recall, recall each his own atrocity, total recall, we have something

we   have   something   left   to   say   to   them   maggots

TWO

ON THE
BEARSKIN
RUG IN FRONT
OF THE FIRE
I CONSTRUCT
THE FOLLOWING
TABLEAU:

I decapitate the ceiling of its ceiling fan. Invert fan, set Great-great-granny atop. Mount her atop. From her mouth drips the pull-chain. Pull it, and out pops the wolf's head, bare in some spots, mange-ridden, rid of teeth, one eye vacant and the other eye boiling. Pull it twice, and out pops the lumberjack, crammed deep his own axe. Set the lights to blazing, the blades to spinning, and Great-great-granny rises like Shiva. Narrate: *A long for the ride.*

Slag crack jaw and withdraw the lathe on which for thirty-some years my scum has collected. Turned. The audience expecting a milkwad, a cherry chrysalis, as promised, the program, platforming. I got a winch-tight wedge heel. You want milky? Narrate: *You want milky? You want mooch?*

The undead shirk, circle shirk in their Bondo-clogged antennae hole. Here's a bosom town on the skids. Here's a big hole in the crush rag where the undead stuff their 1994. Over here, I'm gonna pin up that tongue that used to lick me far and wide and I'm gonna apple soak it and I'm gonna go more red in the face than green. Narrate: *Better. Bitters.*

An Oz fuck. A single red braid encasing the extension cord. I set an emerald top hat on Granddad, and light his beard. A tumbler, the locks betraying. Granddad's spit rolls out to beat the band, and I with a cup try drowning him next. Try wearing my most gingham and my cherriest and carrying a bladder full of yeast. Next, a slide rule. The aged rubber wheels give less. The wind comes up, blade by blade. Not so much rolling as loosening our grip on the boards. Not so much patricide as Granddad's puked up a future for me and I've taken the mop and the rye and the Scottie dog lighter and a sweater and a Valium, and some sort of tranquilizer has stuck into a thigh of someone or another. Narrate: *If the field ripples, be sure the will stays sound.*

Petrified wood, coal in a zirconia duck blind. The kitten in the cat's teeth diary. The dumb luxe hole on the side of a diary. The ice pick pet soup diary. The letter opener. The certificate of lived birth. The no-option papers. The certificate of legalized yolk. The yolk hardened to the plate. The platelets loose in the russet. A sprayed stiff and starched stiff. Narrate: *Oh cuckoo, or pluck. Oh peignoir'd hatchet-faced premise. Who'll you jail for? Who'll notch your belt?*

This is a movie, the old folks at home. Great wide expanses of tulle or wheat or some tune like that. Tits rising, tempers, pistons, a Tommy gun, six notes ascend. That fucking horse what broke my neck heart. Fucking dog, tomboy, might-peaked fucker. Line the tracks up here, for the train, for the body, for the beast that's got his hunter's back, for the sound of sick sick fan tick hearts a'muster. Narrate: *Ahistorical fox, you foxglove, my neck surrounded by your furry expiration.*

Plaque bug, you freestyle out of loose amber, stagger merry onto the bare patch, the Persian carpet without footing. Nothing here can ricochet. Can growl sour mashed split ooze, trash copper, can disgrace an entire township. Narrate: *The sick tab and its mucoid rat are just things said about an unsettled feeling in the gutter.*

A tear disc. An ink-slick handjob. A benzocaine condom tied up in a bow. A benzocaine fuck. A swift fuck, a kiss-less, a deep whisk, a sweep and shuffle. A crow, a morning do. A note from a jack who's no longer livid. His signature, his risk, his pawn on her manuscript worth less than. Narrate: *Living. He's no longer live.*

Just so nail fuck the sofa back. Prop the chair. In the chair's lap, insert a cream thigh. Two. Insert deflations, cheery soldier pop, stiff-lip it. What part of her body is the instigator willing to install? Here my flesh wand, here my sensation of having once been a particular, here my sick ballet stunk of me. What part of the past is annexed? The part with my slick may-I flushing its futures. The part of the cap that sweat through my brow, the part of the skillet that thought so long on harm it rusted through its own extension. What part of these futures fit? None, I swamp in here, I literally gag on my extra waistband. Narrate: *But our daughter would so love to attend your daughter.*

Well. My desire. Has come 'round again. Has and the matchsticks splay. Out my hands, my legs splay out, organs, heart. Splayed on the hearth. I say you "Fuck It," and "Pound Here." It's not him I'm trying to get me. It's them littles. Narrate: *Mares eat oats and does eat oats and little lambs incise me—*

Items not to be touched: Young blonde torso, young black torso, young scarred torso with nipple ring too, young tattooed torso begging touch. Young neck to jaw, young cock on thigh, young hipbone north of lariat, young calf-strung. Do not touch the cowboys, do not touch the movers, do not touch the drywall crew. Do not touch the painters who are coming in the morning. Do not touch him, do not touch his friend, do not touch anyone who sits in this chair across, and do not move the chair imperceptibly closer when he steps into the other room. Not to be touched: the brow, the bent brow, the broken, beaded, furrowed brow. Not with lips, even in a moment of weak and tender love make. Narrate: *Are you young, Mama? Are you a girl?*

Two criminals arranged as one body with four arms and four legs and four thousand slides notched into orifices, and, once orifices filled, notched into skin, roped into hair, wound into ropes used to secure criminals. It is called tenure, it is called rapture, it is called to order and begged to keep happening, no matter what, to never stop happening to consecutive generations of heartsick addendums. Narrate: *I too over the sink in the dark. I too in the red light district of chemical skivvies. Shake, shake, shake, Señora.*

Down so long that down does not even look like up from a braided cell. A string rag band, a sluicing of dull old assembly of dull old limbs, fore to aft, and shin to spinet, a small electric organ, and even the variety show known as legs hooked behind back, ear to thigh, the swift crotch. A diagram in ash and jimmies says here's to fuck it till you reel again. Narrate: *Whatever. Unhhhh.*

The fuckwad brings a sarcastic remark to dinner. He's filleted it, it's raw, he has a chart with which the other guests can identify its succulent measures.

THREE

WOLF SPIDER

Unsacked rice fret into light,
slog pot with your grizzled feel.
Once you had a fine excuse
for a lover. You slammed-gut
swollen sack of piggy laters.

Scalped, then trucked it
with his grease wrought muscle
and found yourself upended
tending to his slag-bit rounds.

The woody slop tripped you up.
In your neutral, in your bug brown,
in your gray freeze hammock.

No rutting, shriek sliver
combing leg from frame.
Now what do you recall,
fatted by your charges?

A tub of blood dilute?
Skunk cabbage marriage?
Promise-style fuck zone, cold flab
flannel pilling. Woozy, yeast stank,
you felt your loathsome way
across the old plank floor.

EARTHWORM

Pin gilt-edged flap to flap, prying
loose the pinched tips. Execute
a sticky hobble; the starch sloughs off.
Here on the graphite slab many degrees colder,
one mustn't drink from the puddle.

Must plastic over against the drone-fry
fluorescence. The bloom on the slide,
one's own AWOL cellular freak. One's own
kept from one by another. The doubled
dotted trim, a reminder second by fierce
tick rank imposter-red second.

That crystal? A sugar,
a salt, an acid.
And oneself
hot with moonshot.

F I S H

Salted wreck. Two-tone disease
fed on dehydrated pest
and chemical-fused utensil.
Record the offense
of the river. Contract
the mutative tools
and with these remove girl
from her bow from boy
from sprit. Oh X it, Y pledge,
graft fin in each reticule
as is your pleasure, food.

Expand your lungs, your liver
and release slick foil memory.
The grade of your history
poisons every fine thing,
so equates lack with luster,
rod with reel, bank with scale.
As you braid into the mouth
the next pink revision.

PEARL

Permanent prenatal nimbus,
whack-skulled and coreless.
A dim sob, your patina. Ductless.
Weep not, but swoon. Adored solder,
head-drilled emissary.

In the privilege tents, you cauterize
a prosthetic heart and fibrillate.

Oh little wine glut.
Oh little about whom little.
Precious gut-fed tumor moon.
Rigged spectral bloodless treasure.
Alluvial dilettante,
dandy parasite.

Replicated endlessly
along the flesh-proud wire.

Kin to the calcified fetus,
you pledge constancy.

F O X

Puff that hindquarter.
In the freeze a bark is wont.
Place sack on stump
and slip trimming from burlap, flat.

Four-cornered bundled. With stripped pink
human inside, or else with chicken
feathers slipping from pores super-red
gooseflesh chicken fringe.

Or else the stump sawn and quartered,
reassembled. Call it the table. Call the family
and 'round they gather. Straight-backed.
A cushion tied to each. Gagged with
cushion, gagging
sweet grease from the nutty wealth.

Or else, wear a fashionable hat,
carry a fashionable stick,
visit a fashionable site
of your own maul.

F L Y

Make thousands of eyes at your prey.
Land with digits, carry your own
syrup with you. Trim
multicolored friction, wave
each of your larvae
on to better things.

The paper's attraction,
its slender depthless promise
to meet you panging. To hang
from its own neck and extend
its own trunk to you, your quick flex,
aforementioned syrup. The match flare
could wizen you. The damp season.
But it isn't, after all, you for the fuckless jelly.

It is six-figured eggs and turncoat.

STINGRAY

Strap on your boots.
On the straps, as though the strops
on which a razor earns its title,
list your abashing glug.

Deterred though you are
by a snigger in the cervix.

Lift yourself by the tail you've poached.
Spoon to the fickle you're cinched.
However can you be blamed
for having one head in traction,
and one beneath the neat
rock bottom, sea box, calcifying panic?

Can it be any wonder,
when the bullets so plentiful?
Fungal crumb askew, speckled
ethics in a warm knot, a wurst?

Do not think your occupation
so small it doesn't somehow
commit to the horror.

W I N D

Settle, why don't you, for that fainéant turbine.
That suckling plateau rat. In cold lung hours,
you make your plaint known, central,
stench-hiss through the grate
of every last sinner.

Singular moan, catfight veteran,
no shame in your hobble. Where once
you kept the word of God, you now spasm
with macrocosmic glut. Weighted,
intoning nothing less

than the shape of string to come.

So who will shed you? Will cast
you off, sack you down the ravine
where girls were sawn
their feet from their sex,
their get up from go.
You told no one.
You hogged it all close

to your quivering gloss.

THE MISSER

Here's her wrapper, a plastic casket.
A blue box zoned, its scab handles wagging.
She was shod, that much is clear.
Blonded. Bound. Among their rods
and tackle, no one
pinned, no one armed.
Drug tide.

Here's her shot face,
rounding the bleak box, rosing
the fat side of grief.

Here's her dead
survived by the amnesiac version,
roped into her growth-spurt
bone box.

They claim to have found her
skinned sack weathering the desert.
A wet rag fin bought them complicity.
A VHS bunco, a hate flab
members only minor scale.

A box. No one on this side of the aisle.

HORSE

The womb, a tick tock, a shrapnel-bearing croc.
Daylight scum rigging, turpentine swilling.
Next the cog, glutted on tubal despair,
freak-white on the far side
of her bone-bright cell.
Shorn as her familiar.

Lip, carnelian bitch-froth.
Airless hiss, worn in a scythe.
Skin glove laced tight, a wax doll
mildewed sinking limb.
Great hole full of mouth holes.
Eye holes, cavities and sugar cubes.

The hog box hums beneath fetid petticoat.
Cats have been among the beds.

Spoon up the fatty stars
from their reeking swarming broth.
Pin the siren through her thorny pap.
A figurehead for your toxic rick.
Claim her fussing milk-stained bairns,
little men precious in their dampened fleece.

A stainless gothic quill
stakes each retina in its rubber globe.

A Death's brow pearl

for every last admirer,

for every winsome brute.

CORD OF WOOD

Livid. Warp-stacked, scenting, known.
The law whelps up around you, chip-shot
bandage, Talleyrand in muck boots.
Oh prince pauper land whore.

Oh sometimes actual nature.

Tango tangle, a spike in your punch.
Colonial handle fancy
pants, or else loose-limbed cuddle
your militant legacy,
crown your science sow.

Operetta! Dank flounce!

Starlet! Starlet fist in your pappy,
turning the charm dim-watt meat.
Fain blond crib, Norwegian
shrug song, soft
on crime, on dandlings
and sea geese. Throw open your

gates to just anyone,
keep those home fires fir and glint.

Here, in the future, your salute's full of moth rot.

S I L K

Wormless fiber casket, raveled,
fostering no brief hickey between
pap and flank, but end-to-ended,
looming, you grace every brothel,
betrothal, friction-snagged union.
Wed to yourself, spoon-tart, draped
without mercy.

Once, home to a busy fella,
you scoured yourself. Found yourself
excrete and sour. Now, nothing cleans
your clock. Whistle drunk, spilled upon,
hagged out the tower at daybreak.
Shed interiors.

Tally up, death squad of one.
Thousands of heels shatter,
shat in the gutter,
thousand sour lashings.

Give your handsome carriage to any cop
outside the limo's crunch,
and find yourself red
in the carpet,
shaved to the bone,
worn with the contempt of the age.

L U M P   O F   C O A L

Potential mastectomy, surface-choking
bleak bulge. History of all things dead,
you read rag after rag—
teenage psychics and crowned prince.

You outwit. No one sees you
undergo as if by fire, or recognizes
your gunked-out train. You slink into
the last breath of the abductee.
In selfless moments,

pen a note to her parents. Stampless, heartless,
grim-centered, blood-candied.
You take an uncle, and rub him out
in the dirt, skull-lit, his dungaree.

Later, hum it, *I will feel a glow just thinking* . . .

At 3 a.m., a loveless independence day
will scuttle off your back,
back into the core,
you money to burn, time
to burn, where nothing's slick
but your own fat biding. Oracle
of raw deal
in the toe of some nip's

cloud-cuckoo, no one ever inserts you

like they said they would.

The fuckwad says: My muckle of muff the umbrella-headed guinea fowl. She eats not, she wants not, she shad me.

FOUR

PUNISHMENT

The punishment came in the form of a femur. A shrill
cat scratch flag of bone. The punishment came
in the form of a swell-gutted viewfinder, slick cards
spinning, spoke spooking, vulgar nostalgic. Soap
sock spastic nail gun frantic tag fist and plaguing
the socket. Swish of the tongue tooth call, swish fake,
but failsafe. Hissy fitted. Studded PVC wishbone.

The darling punishment. A graph grown boot knife
in the back of the neck. In the sorry cleft. A boot
in the neck, a blue-fisted kisser. A weft slug, a slit
knit kill prone. The punishment was well deserved.

The punishment came in the form of a femur
from one's own body. Hefted, weighted, hulked back.
Came link-fisted, augmented, tampered to perfection. With
an aerosol can. A sting fix, a shrewd eye. Cuffs, cables.
Torch, panic button. Practice, fuckwad, nothing personal.

Fuckwad, history's cockroach, progeny cockroach,
wax-sealed silk-legged multi-beast. Famine-sexed
premonitory landlubber. I mean you, dreg bug, coyly
sluicing the grotto. Face over face, mask ecstatic
exo-spiel. Trade wind winced you once, and you,
orphan by choice, heavy lifting plug holing pack wracking
bleach fiend, lesson learned.

Here your
freak

In the wake of most revolutions, a pug will yet be attached to your teat

tassel comfort lodge. Here your calf
collection, plaster cast mistress improvements, net bearing
stumps, sanitized plow proof. Fact fickle, your memoir
slugs wan into the room, velvet fug parted, rank
chicken wing mattress scuttle, rank robe parted, hissing.

Sings it high the old tune, the fuckwad, humming, French
and bawd, humming, *This the bitch who waits on the rug,*
fire-spooked, slipper-gagged, this the bitch who keeps
her head, bears her head and broods.

The fuckwad has placed her in the room with the knife.

Behind one-way glass he zooms. Watch her pollywog doing.

First will she slice out her hundred tongues. Her beaded, beetled,

work-wise tonguing. Then nine-quandrant cross-

section skull brain scalp and face.

Oh, she gives out unwise teeter. But

The real sleety
meaty vacancy

the dermoid void. Drain her winning doubt,

chain her slick padding, and still winks her wile under the table.

Then face it, face plow and she zeroes the camera: *I would not
wash my horse in men.* She foams. A soap escapes her. A single

little bronze baked shoe escapes her. A root, she carves it.

Rare, she says. She runs her hand across the lens, and sap scums

the flick-fouled screen.

Say like you mean what you mean spasm so badly wanted

to ratchet. To mean down your throat with this cold cut

rag. For six hours, privy fact clog, I'm not at all exaggerating,

for six hours I read over   the fuckwad's

reasonable statements. | I set my jaw with | Wallet-fisted cure

face. Salt-pressed sick song. | the fuck squall and | Every ugmo

dictation preserved and   jar-shipped to

exhibit.

What has looking got him? Bacterial scale male seahorse

stuffed in the pocket of my seahorsey frame. My grand,

my gracious reception of your plugging away. It doesn't

matter that the wooziness fells me. Doesn't matter that

I just now went from spit to fracture.

Here are his fertility rights: to keep his head on straight

after the thing itself.

                              To keep his wiggle in its worm.

The fuckwad has her caged, rat-style. He sends babies chute face,
chute face. She chews face, face plowed, baby after baby.
He box checks, he checks box, he slots baby, he plows.
Then cokes. He offers to coke her. She nuzzles
a baby, opens her face.

> All I want is a lot
> of babies and a
> lot of money; you
> made me so pay it

What's that? Out there in the yards, a passel of fetal cell
flanked fans are gunning. The fuckwad hits the lab lights. He
croons it, *I see the love light in your eyes*, he dimmer switches,
gnaws. The raw babies glow.
They're props, they fidget, they stack
neatly in the corner, and crown.

Take note and heed. My drab elastic shackle worried the bone
to dart. Poison tipped present day cervix fasting, preparatory.
Ugly Park looms and I file its gates. Specific access: Trees
denied, fur denied, zing and whoosh denied, all water denied.
Dark denied, particle-free oxygens denied, nutrients denied.
Girls, boys, tom-toms, flowers, spoons, ink, porcelain, fruit,
tone, flint, exploration, and tonic fetal compass denied.

I have a plot of land for you.
I have it trimmed-edge and furnished.
Each blade measured, each puncture
depth predicted, never

> The next time you survey your land,
>
> your land will accommodate your skull

more than necessary. Wake you, each minor second, and witness
the pestilent staccato of a million minor infractions loosed.

Down to the boneyard, then. And dig your corpse and
with pliers pluck out one after the other its teeth and plant
them in my very own mouth. Your happy clackers to mitt
my sweater sleeves, and when it's time to light the way,
your gall. My gal, Mister. Gussy in your worm-drenched
nerve, and quick with the pink Catawba.

Hammer-ended kissy face, I chap your coffin and bag
your tootsies. Sure you have the numbers one through
one hundred. Sure the musical renditions, the Chinese
artifacts, all facts, all figures, all spittle-scripted marginalia.
I've got naught, that's the beaut. I've got a nickel and

a hangnail. I've got your nails   catalogued, ready
for stringing. Underside each,   a grave grub, and in each
grub, one of the many letters
you never came out with.

> I am talking dirty
> to you like you are
> the only one in the
> room

Oh, did I mention? We got ourselves a renaissance of can't.

61

Where to flesh the bone?   Skin score, nettle suck.

Dotted fissure   promise slicker. The

fuckwad, hardly dead, spoons   With your licker caught   in a morgue bin.

It's a grief rebate, he says. Says   in the zipper   she, *Cut not, want not,*

click not

into place a shiv where a wellbeing were.

They'll say you've snapped, princess.

They'll say so.

The fuckwad wants to compare nonfeelings. Wick
stumper cesspool torquing slack bastion cracks wide.
I hoof it through Ugly Park to the fixit. A salve please,
an antibacterial spill theorem. Freak tag my chart please,
my lick please, my rigged stop heart thwack. Slushing.

A swab please.
inside the gates close,
perched. Chairs banal,
peace farce. Oh pill
zone

Whichever pen you use
to sign, your own
blood issues

Outside the crow birds on gates and
the astrologers fluffed and ready,
savannah ink blot stone fed
me. Still me stinking ripe face gone

proof.

Slow me and fence it. I hock shop I gold play I leaking
valuables. There is a window, roll call, a vile plastic stack.

The book is right, everyone is miscarrying. Friends, geese, friends,
thieves' friends, goody people, ferret-faced blonde hags, limbed
and limbless, lank and fatted over with numb.

Over the toilet, but under her rag hole, extending

a plastic cup to catch that   THING SHE WERE

SUPPOSED TO LOVE.   *Shall I love me*

my thready discharge?

> For each director who uses
> my miscarriage for that smug
> apocalypse, I will grease a
> head with vegetable
> shortening and shove it
> through the bars of my krill-
> coated slit

In Ugly Park, they slam.   They shrug her up

outside her door, which   she cannot fist loose,

shriek s'pose. They call in   the fuckwad

and swift rig tamp stand   ask him to apply

the pamphlet about   BITCHES

WHO ABORT, regardless. The fuckwad says it: *Oh my merry lamb, oh my lambykin,*

oh my

*satin-riddled whoopee pie. Put a thumb of fatty here, take a brisk
there, bite it, lick it, suck it, swallow this. Oh my one in four, my
maybe one in two, or each's every, and your little gran too.*

Then shuck her slit gown and ship her out in the red hood.

Check me, fun wig candy spun ringlet red to ultra,
a peignoir smocked breast tattered ladder stitch ribbon
greased up hem, reflective glasses from the chop cop.
Nothing, though, till you see my stickware.

Dinner's under the sheet. Squirmy, fixed yet. A ring

I   am   now   your   own   private   spook   brigade

of salt, charred some, table's edge. I'll have you know
it's a stew.

A grim little sliver that fits the ignition, a grape-scented
fibrous gallon of puncture. A tutelage ripe in fringe
sanitation, don't you tell me I never you nothing you did.

Vagrant sack of fats; grim juicy; sour metal rodent;

spank of loamiest factor. The chamber pot composes

a bill of sale.

The fuckwad, I heard him a'singing his organs to heaven.

One by one, little children. They were not a bastard,

but

otherwise.

They were

> No matter what box you're offered, you will X out the following,
> and your eye will appear to be blackened:

of

Frankenstein foot and golem

toothed. They claw-stomped the fuckwad's shag, and he

was so glad of 'em, he never saw it coming.

What? My c-u-t? My cutty pie? It did release a feather,

and in it DNA.

FIVE

THE BID FOR PAIN

Crack an egg, drain the white into a boiled jar, suck the white into a plastic syringe just out of its sterile wrapper, a medicine syringe. Insert the syringe into my vagina. Plunge the egg white into, that is spurt, that is up. A muscular tunnel replete with mucoid protein. Direct my vagina to the cock. The tip, the furnishing pulses. I admit the cock and encourage its performance. I dismiss the cock and tip upward. I manufacture my clitoris, I seize and spasm. My uterus, crane. Hip cranked, and thus, rathood. By no other means, I assure.

How does this procedure become my face? Fetal cells cross the blood-brain barrier. The uterus need not travel for its vast field meets me there. But how does this procedure become my face?

I present a meat oven, cracked wide by the uncanny photographer X. Rotting, I wear this organic coffin awkwardly. I am a convivial herpes, by which 96% are infected, but most have yet to manifest lesions. I am a greater percentage bacteria, a series of plagiarized infestations. How dare we call ourselves *self* and sign my name to these documents. How dare we gather on my face in a parade formation.

Still, I rate pain. I rate my own operation, and a room in which to distend my anus. My contraction machine, my flared labia, my regret that I cannot attend this event, am rushed out in the surge of field. Fielding. My middle face banished, *homo sacer*, neither sacrifice nor dead meat. A mother mask was stitched to my raw zone. It was a mistake, but it was not wholly successful.

THE MANNER IN WHICH PAIN BECOMES ME

1. A fistula wrote a pamphlet. He claimed that the males of the species were stalking him. He claimed to be ignorant of their whereabouts at the time of the writing. He found a pair of their shoes clutched in the arms of a sodden *Homo erectus*. He compared the soles of the shoes to the prints outside his window. He found their tissues in his garden. "What they want," said the fistula, "is a repeat performance." He claimed that the male of the species was doing it for his own good. He claimed that the theater was musty, its curtains vulgar, and he emptied its costume loft into a bin marked *rubbish*.

2. A calcified fetus wrote a pamphlet. It claimed to have been present at the hour the siren began deafening the village. It claimed to be a black woman's problem. It claimed to be a Ukrainian grandmother's snuff box. In its humble opinion, it couldn't imagine a more spacious turf. It refused to give up its box seats at the opera. To be jolly, it said, one must never cede.

3. A fashion victim wrote a pamphlet. He claimed to have inadvertently stitched his heart to a batwing sweater sleeve. He claimed that the sweater's waist wasn't cinched tightly enough. He claimed that the heart on its sleeve was the human heart, meaning that it came from a human and it produced human-leaked AB blood whenever an emotion walked by. He drew a flow chart to illustrate from which races the various blood types could be drained. At the end of the chart, he drew a multicolored figure with two breasts and a codpiece. He labeled it *good persons*. Halfway through the pamphlet, he claimed it had just occurred to him that he meant what he was saying. He claimed that there was a valuable wetness filming his eye, and that his locks were renegade. Rummaging through his neighbor's garbage, he found a dead puppy. He claimed that his neighbors were not amusing, that the only ones laughing were the garbage men.

4. A ml of Botox wrote an entry in a pink diary that locked with a pink plastic key. The diary contained twenty-eight blisters. Only one blister was marked. The ml of Botox claimed an advantage over other compositions. It claimed that it alone could produce that endless series of inexpressions, each of which would correspond to an inarticulable synaptic disaster.

PAIN BEAK-PECKS A FIGURINE

Daily, I bleach and refigure my middle face. I know that this is WRONG, but I do it anyway. I frame it with poison sumac and dare it to swell. On either side of my middle face, I know that I should not send my professor an anatomically correct doll wrapped in my F*CK GLACÉ world tour T-shirt, or commission a hand-wrought copper flight recorder in which to store my cream manes. Late nights, when I hear my father come to bed, I pray for a migraine so that I might sever before my parents ape each other's genitals. If I were a good girl, says the sky pilot, I would pray in the morning as well as at bedtime. But even my porcelain merry-go-round, lame and legless, knows how the fist will shoot. I relic pain, I treat my skullcap, and fan out my beard.

EXTRATERRESTRIAL PAINSAKE

I left that world a'weeping, sings the fuckwad. *I left that world my lone dog howling, I left that world my bed surrounded by sugar lumps and glassy knobs. I left that world to meet my* maker, *I left that world my sin skinned and fat run in the basin.* Which is how we know the fuck remains. His teat slammed in the door will give him away. His brow pimpled with exposure. He hangs on the world with all twenty brittle nails, yellow, fungal, earthy. He hisses a carbon sack that damps the room. His files are on display in the Natural History Rape Museum. Alongside his death mask, cast in plaster, his cat in plaster, his mate pumped full of plaster. His sweetmeat detailed on the program, a chorus of.

ACKNOWLEDGMENTS

42 Opus: [All I want is a lot of babies and a lot of money; you made me so pay it]

Action, Yes!: The Bid for Pain, The Manner in Which Pain Becomes Me, Pain Beak-Pecks a Figurine, Extraterrestrial Painsake

Black Warrior Review: Cord of Wood, Pearl, [I am talking dirty to you like you're the only one in the room], Wolf Spider

Dancing Bear Reader: Horse

Delirious Hem: On the Bearskin Rug in Front of the Fire I Construct the Following Tableau: (excerpts)

Fou: [In the wake of most revolutions a pug will yet be attached to your teat], [The real sleety meaty vacancy]

Grist: On the Bearskin Rug in Front of the Fire I Construct the Following Tableau: (excerpts)

Gurlesque: The New Grrly, Grotesque, Burlesque Poetics: [Advice will be heeded even as you attempt to head strong / headstrong], Horse, [I am now your own private spook brigade], [Whichever pen you use to sign, your own blood issues]

MiPoesias: [The man in your life will exercise his fink till it wail], Punishment

No Tell Motel: [When you lie down you get up again and there are fleas as well as bedbugs], [Advice will be heeded even as you attempt to head strong / headstrong], [I am now your own private spook brigade], [No matter what box you're offered, you will X out the following, and your eye will appear to be blackened:]

Shampoo: [For each director who uses my miscarriage for that smug apocalypse, I will grease a head with vegetable shortening and shove it through the bars of my krill-coated slit], [I am boring you to death; I am boring into you]

Smoking Glue Gun: [I hated myself in your womb from conception], [I set my jaw with the fuck squall and], [You put me in this dress, I'm just wearing it. Externally.]

Today's Poetry: [I am boring you to death; I am boring into you]

Verse Daily: Cord of Wood, Pearl, [I am talking dirty to you like you're the only one in the room]

ABOUT THE AUTHOR

Danielle Pafunda is the author of *Natural History Rape Museum* (Bloof Books, 2013), *Manhater* (Dusie Press, 2012), *Iatrogenic: Their Testimonies* (Noemi Press, 2010), *My Zorba* (Bloof Books, 2008), and *Pretty Young Thing* (Soft Skull Press, 2005). Her poems have appeared in three editions of *The Best American Poetry*. Her work has been anthologized in *Beauty Is a Verb: The Poetry of Disability* (Cinco Puntos Press, 2011), *Gurlesque: The New Grrly, Grotesque, Burlesque Poetics* (Saturnalia Books, 2010), and *Not for Mothers Only: Contemporary Poems on Child-Getting & Child Rearing* (Fence Books, 2007). She is Assistant Professor of English at the University of Wyoming.

PRAISE FOR
DANIELLE PAFUNDA

Lifting a page from Plath's book of tricks, Pafunda comes out swinging.

—*Publishers Weekly*

Some poets take language out for a long, leisurely lunch and a stroll. Danielle Pafunda drags language out of bed in the middle of the night and takes it on a desperate mission through the war-torn house of the body.

—*The Lesser of Two Equals*

Pafunda strokes at and strums gender constructions, exposing the mossy dungeon that holds this consensual social structure up. [. . .] As much as these poems rail against the structures that have shaped their speakers, their power comes from fully inhabiting that debasement, however uncomfortable or torturous it may be. In that, we can see the full promise of the grotesque at work.

—Sueyuen Juliette Lee, *Constant Critic*

Her sexual and social frankness will remind you of the mid-period Anne Sexton, for like Sexton, Pafunda is rebelling against a system which has a name for everything except the things most important to a human, not to mention a woman. —Kevin Killian

I was utterly blown away by Pafunda's unique use of language and creation of a kind of science-fiction world that I have never before seen in poetry. [. . .] vivid, intoxicating, and forever disturbing, poems which will be nearly impossible for a reader to forget. —Kristin Abraham, *H_NGM_N*

A Plath-descendant, Pafunda's speakers' polemic attitudes build a cage around opponents' gazes. —*So to Speak Journal*